SINGLE PARENTING: The ultimate guide on how to become the best parent to your kids.

Richard Walter

Table of contents

Chapter 1

The Transition And New Circumstance

The shift and new situation - traveling along the route of the lone parent
You are also developing and changing during this process. You will recognize it, your kids will know and witness it, as will others. This is another shift you and everyone around you have to cope with as well, on top of everything else.

You could also feel worried, lonely, and furious or elicit similar feelings in your child/family. Again this is a completely typical and natural behavior.

"Seeing things from the child's point of view. This is not simply all about you either. Try to view things through the eyes of your kid occasionally and entire new realms of understanding and possibility will open for you.

"A new road and survival strategy for single parents - rewards and difficulties

We have discussed a lot in theory about what happens to you when presented with these scenarios. Now we move to the more practical WHAT DO I DO NOW, NEXT, IN MY CASE TYPE OF QUESTIONS?

"SETTLING IN AS INDIVIDUALS AND A NEW FAMILY UNIT

Challenges:

There are so many, that it is certainly feasible to create one complete book on this subject alone. We are deciding to take a bit less 'negative' approach to this. Rather concentrate on the method and result than the surrounding, complications, causes, uphill fights, and hurdles every one of us could personally confront. Here are some examples:

Getting everything done, on schedule, being where you need to be, doing what you have to do, and keeping sane through it all.

Finding the financial means (food, boarding/housing, transportation, food, clothes and providing needs of life, safe place to stay, live and play) Baby-sitting and daycare, job and income, support, and other family-related issues.

Emotionally sustaining your kids, while and despite your world crumbling before your eyes. Being and supplying the steadiness while you do not believe you can or have it in you.

Coping with loss and transition and the new tasks and obligations of being a lone custodian and principal caregiver, provider, and leader of the family.

Rewards: Life does go on! You can do it!

Together with your kids, you are going on reclaiming and creating your life together. You are embracing your future with a good attitude, optimism, and a plan of action. Renewed connection, deeper love, and caring relationship with your kids.

Chapter 2

Organizing

Challenges: Tension, tension, harsh words, conflict, disputes, disagreements, quality of family life together, synergy, emotions that are rampant and patience running thin, anger at the tiniest little thing. Lack of concentration and direction

Rewards: How you as a family can join together and work through difficulties, caring and supporting each other, even when the going gets tough, making the links and connections even stronger than before. Talking about things that are challenging and how you are dealing may be an eye-opener, sharing opinions and solutions is incredibly powerful!

Providing stability, order, regularity, routine and a strong foundation amongst uncertainty is a great duty BUT also an incredible chance to reconnect with one other.

Getting, staying, and keeping everyone else on track and organized, fed, dressed, taken care of, on time, where they need to be when they need to be, in clean clothing, and remaining sane in the process can be quite the task for any single parent. The advantage is that it offers you the chance to inspire, engage and mobilize your kids into and in your family unit. They take part in establishing and molding their happiness, family life, and future. That is a wonderful prize. A fresh start and starting, possibilities, and potential. Keep focused on the good as opposed to dwelling in and upon the past. It is of essential significance that anybody and everyone remain connected, have a voice, speak out, communicate effectively and check in with each other often. This is the ideal time to aid in beginning the healing process, strengthening the links and connections between parents and kids, individually and collectively as a family unit.

You are the authority and disciplinarian in the family unit. Demand and earn respect, trust, and honesty. Be fair, transparent, and consistent. Do not overreact and make some guidelines so that you all can live within this new scenario. Organizing and personalizing your life the way you want it. Who gets to do what, and when? Sports and after-school activities, weekends and hobbies, and more can be discussed and decided together. The lone parent, guardian, and champion of course have the last say and opinion.

Do all in your power to develop your children's originality and personality. Everyone has something that makes them special NEVER FORGET THAT. Encourage their self-sufficiency and independence. Let them do chores around the house, take control of their lives and stop acting like victims, try and play guilt games or manipulate, disobey, rebel, or act out. Teach children to respect you, each other, and others at all times.

How does your family (new) manage disagreement, stress, and crisis? Are there verbal disputes in the household?
Can you still love and care for each other, despite the problems and or words that you are having? How do you keep grounded and connected?
Are there chances for the family and you and the kids, one-on-one to discuss how

they feel, what they want, worries, and disagreements?

Chapter 3

New Family Unit

Challenges and rewards: letting go of the old and embracing the new, also involved moving beyond the past, breaking ties, and moving on. As mentioned earlier, this causes a lot of stress and anxiety (especially for the kids) (especially for the kids). It is journeying into the unknown, uncertain, and un-chartered waters and territory.

As a member of this new family situation and context, unit, everyone has a role to play and a contribution to make. Whether you are in an only child or multiple children situation, you will feel the weight of this one on your shoulder. These children's lives are entrusted and loaned to you to champion, enable, empower and foster. You are all they've got. You are the one left behind. Some children cope with changes, loss, and upheaval better than others. NO TWO KIDS ARE THE SAME.

Dealing with fights, rebellious behavior, bad grades, and even isolation and detachment, can be hard at times - especially if they are your children. You can try and compensate for the missing parent but never replace or bad mouth. Teach and model respect, forgiveness, and consideration, no matter how tough the situation. They are now looking to you for guidelines and direction.

If you have an only kid, you may consider this as your ONE chance to make things right. Do not place too much pressure and expectation on any of you. Enjoy and cultivate, and strengthen your friendship, link, and connection.

Being over-protective is the true risk here. Attachment and concern are fairly frequent as kids become the center of our being and life. They are the reason we live. Sometimes we as single parents might take this too far and need to pull back slightly to enable our kids to live their lives, explore and define who they are, outside of us and the family unit.

THESE ARE THE FIVE "S" ways to cope with an only child:

Self-definition - who are you, where do you belong and you are not the ONLY people in this home or the world that cares. Self-assured and important, self-absorbed and selfish should not be accepted. Appreciation and concern for others have to be taught at home, in the family, even and particularly if there is an only kid in the unit.

Socialization - connecting with people, beside oneself is vital, particularly youngsters their age, friends and other neighborhood adults and families may also assist. Kids must be and act their age!

Age - Appropriate Actions

Always remember that your kid did not seek to be put in this predicament. Whether you have babies, teenagers, or young adults in the house (early, mid or late adolescence) and/or kids who would want to assert their independence and use this as an opportunity to move out on their own, there are considerations, challenges, and rewards. IT DOES NOT ALL HAVE TO BE BAD!

Uncertainty, disagreement, and antagonism may be quite palpable when kids start to become more and more self-sufficient and autonomous. It might be hard to let this and not be over-protective, BUT YOU HAVE TO LET GO.

As a single parent, you are the one helping your child/children shape who they are, become, and will be. Their character and qualities will begin establishing themselves, both physically and socially. Values, habits, and desires change with time as people become more autonomous. This may both make a parent grin and grimace with quick anxiety. You could be questioning yourself whether your kid (and you) are ready for the trials of life and the real world outside the home.

While this growing apart and separation occur over time, it may be difficult for both partners and produce discomfort even confrontation and conflict when all these 'wills' meet.

Yet, it does not all have to be an ongoing conflict, there is much that you can do to develop independence and get along living under one roof.

Energy, attitude, and conduct are frequently the first tell-tale signals that something is unusual and changing. Negativity, revolt and even experimentation that does not always meet with your approval could be occurring.

Values, risks, and observation are the single parent's arsenal for coping with this. Accountability and consequences, discipline and sensitivity, understanding, and a firm, the consistent stance can be life savers as well.

In everything strive to work towards retaining and nurturing that good relationship and connection that you have and always give that soft place to fall and return home to for them. Being thoughtful of you and your siblings, as well as family life in general, are all vital.

You have to educate your kids that they are part of the family and have a role to perform, contributions to make, and rules to respect.

Chapter 4

Consequences Of Single Parenting

Being a single parent involves many difficult challenges. It's even harder than it looks. Single parents deal with challenges all day, every day. Many of those challenges arise from being not only single but a parent. There are children to care for and take care of. And because you are the only parent, everything you do carries greater weight.

No matter what you do, as a single parent, you must think of its effect on your children. You must be diligent in keeping up with their activities and their thoughts as they grow up in a single-parent home. The biggest challenge of being a single parent is the effect of your status on your children.

The transition to a single-parent family is difficult for kids. They may feel abandoned or insecure. They may feel isolated and different from other kids, even if there are more single-parent families than ever before.

Your children may resent you for the loss of your spouse, or they may have unresolved issues with the missing parent. As a single parent, it's your job to keep them talking about what's going on with them and what they think. Even though they may resist, you need to urge them to speak to you about their concerns, their anxieties, and their anger.

And you need to let them know they're all right. They're typical kids despite their circumstances. They aren't accountable for the alteration, and they don't have to make up for it. You should give them as normal a childhood as possible and be a role model. Even when kids don't behave that way, they look to you as their model of what a grown-up is and does.

Your kids need to know you're there for them, no matter what. You have a busy schedule trying to earn a living and manage the household. But you must never be too busy for your children. Even when you are in financial trouble, the job can't take priority over the kids. They need to know how important they are to you. They need to know you love them more than anything else. You're going to have to build a new relationship with your children. As a single parent, you're the only source of affection and guidance in the home. Even if you weren't close before, you're going to have to get close now. One smart approach to achieve it is to do plenty of enjoyable family activities.

Another technique that will aid the entire family is to give particular jobs to your children that will help keep the home operating properly. Giving them responsibilities will make them feel that they belong and that they are valued. It will also provide children with a feeling of achievement essential to establishing a healthy self-image.

Single parents need to confess that they need support and then receive aid. You can't accomplish everything by yourself. Trying to may harm your health, your mood, and your relationships with your children. Getting to know your neighbors is a terrific approach to identifying individuals who can assist you care for the kids while you must be gone. Neighbors may also assist with home repairs and yard chores.

Your neighbors may also be adult companions and role models for your children, but you must be cautious. Get to know your neighbors well before you allow your children to be alone with them. Remember that the world is a more hazardous place than it was when you were a youngster. There's no replacement for sound parental discretion.

Time is the enemy when you're a single parent. You probably have to work, and that means being outside the house a lot. Unless you have help, it also means your children may spend a lot of time at home alone. You'll need to take additional measures and spell down particular regulations every when you're not there.

Children who are alone a lot are exposed to drugs and criminal conduct. Gang activity is skyrocketing. You'll have to find a means to watch your kids when you're not home. This challenging task must be handled head-on or your children may pay for it with their own lives.

You may have a struggle with your children's views regarding you as well. They may blame you for their circumstances or believe you're not doing things appropriately. They may not show you the respect you desire and expect. And kids may feel deceived if they can't attend important occasions like birthdays, PTA meetings, parent-teacher conferences, recitals, and other activities that parents generally attend. These time demands are particularly onerous for single parents. If you can't make the time to make at least some of these events, it's time to have a conversation with the boss. Maybe you can work out a specific work schedule or complete part of your job at home. If you can't find a solution with your existing employer, you may need to explore alternative more flexible working arrangements. If both are impossible, your children must know and understand why you can't be with them. Be honest. They'll understand the truth better than no explanation at all.

It's important to remember that you can't just give time to your kids. It must be quality time that helps them grow and mature. They need to know that you love them and that you need them. Never give them the idea that they're a burden to you. Tell them often how much you love them. Listen to them. Ask them questions and listen to their answers. Show your interest in them as individuals. Even when time is limited, you can make the time you spend with them special and positive. It's worth the hassle. And your reward is the love and respect of well-behaved, responsible children.

Even when life deals you and your children a bad hand, you can make a life together enjoyable and productive. You can build healthy relationships with your kids and watch them become happy, productive young adults.

Despite the many hard challenges of being a single parent, you must always maintain your perspective and honor the most important priorities. It won't always be hard or unpleasant. You'll have many happy times and lots of love and laughter in your single-parent family as long as you keep a healthy positive attitude and keep on working toward a better life for yourself and your children.

Chapter 5

The Effects Of Single Parenting

Over the past several decades, there's been tremendous growth in the number of single-parent families. As you would imagine, the number of children in single-parent families has climbed as well. Many people feel that separation and divorce are highly awful for growing children, but others claim that nothing's worse for kids than continual disagreements and even violence in the family.

Social scientists have come to contradictory opinions on the good and negative implications of solitary parenting. Some research finds that living with a single parent leads to poor self-worth for the children. Others find no consequences different from two-parent homes.

It's apparent, however, that single parents can make all the difference in helping their children adjust and manage the move to a single-parent family. How single parents cope with their children at this time may influence family dynamics for the future and impact the well-being of both parent and kid.

Here are a few ways the newly-single parent might be a good supporting influence for their new family.

1. Help your children understand why you are now single.

Before a separation or divorce, the odds are that the family life wasn't very nice. The youngsters may have overheard conflicts or observed personal violence that you don't know about. It's also probable that you weren't as attentive to their sentiments as you could have been if you hadn't been going through so much yourself.

Children who don't comprehend the facts sometimes think that they are the reason for their parent's difficulties. Now that the fireworks are passed, it's time, to be honest with them. You don't have to go into graphic detail, but you do need to let them realize that they are not guilty of the break-up. Without criticizing the absent parent, tell as much as you can about the core dispute between you and why you couldn't work it out. Your transparency and honesty will help them put everything in perspective and will tell them you appreciate their sentiments. Hopefully, this will help diminish any resentments they may be harboring towards you.

2. Spend more time with your children.

You've all gone through a really hard period. Tensions during the break-up may have been strong, and your children may have been aware of and impacted by the stress. They presumably are extremely accustomed to yelling, fighting, and chilly silences. They know animosity well.

Now that you're single and your household is growing more secure, it's time to spend some time with your kids. Doing activities together helps re-establish communications and allows you to get to know each other beyond the stress and strain of the previous existence.

Take time to chat with them about your aspirations and dreams. Ask them about theirs. Plan and embark on holidays, weekend getaways, and fast outings to the beach or wildlife preserve. Have a special family night to "celebrate" the week's successes. The important thing is spending time together to help heal old wounds and build new healthy relationships. It will produce a happier, healthier family.

3. Become part of your community.

Single parents have busy lives and many responsibilities. Depending on the age of your children, they may be able to help. But you must locate local help. Get to know your neighbors. Where they have children near your kids' ages, encourage them to play together.

Ask your neighbors for help when you need it. Don't be too proud to ask for help. You have neighbors who'll be more than happy to help you out with some babysitting or household chores. Neighborhood kids may want to earn a few extra dollars by helping you in your yard. And don't just ask for help, get involved. Take part in neighborhood and community activities. Volunteer, as a family, to participate in and contribute to blocking parties, neighborhood flea markets and yard sales, community watch programs, and other planned events.

It will assist both you and your children create new connections and protect you from feeling alone or lonely following the huge changes you've gone through.

4. Give your youngsters new experiences.

Your kids may be having a tough time, particularly if their time is split between parents. They may be attempting to adapt to a new school and establish new acquaintances. Life may feel overwhelming to them right now. It's crucial that kids feel that life is still an adventure, and they that belong.

Be sure to question them about what they did whilst gone and do not, under any circumstances, use it as the time to trash your ex. Show your interest in what your kids did and what they achieved. Encourage kids to engage in activities for children, join local sports teams, and discover new things. Keep them engaged in the broader world so that they don't get self-absorbed and overwhelmed by their concerns.

5. Let your children grow up with you.

Children need to feel that they have successes, just like the rest of us. You may boost their sentiments of achievement by giving them responsibilities. Assign them particular responsibilities in the home, and then leave the tasks to them. Don't oversee or criticize. Let them fail, and learn, on their own. But do applaud them when they do a good job. Let them know how much you appreciate their aid and how essential they are to your family. And attempt to locate a job for each kid that is visible to and supportive of the family unit.

6. Balance your life by prioritizing your life.

Single parents can be overwhelmed by responsibilities and the things that must be done after a breakup. You must understand how to spend your time to make life better for everyone, including you! If your career is too demanding, you may need to find something new so that you can concentrate on your family. If financial commitments are burdensome, maybe a new job's not the solution. Perhaps attempting to negotiate a different working schedule with your supervisor will be the key.

Begin to think about and create family schedules that are flexible enough for those inevitable unexpected events yet structured enough that your bases are covered. And add leisure and family entertainment to your calendar. Let your children help you design a schedule. This will be another chance for some great chat and to get to know each other better. You never know, your children may have some great ideas that will make everyone's life easier.

7. Make decision-making a family affair.

Now that you're a single parent, it may be tempting to rule with an iron fist. But that would be a mistake. Your kids need the reassurance of knowing you respect and need them. When decisions about the home or family need to be made, include them in the process. Help them comprehend your decision-making criteria and the advantages and downsides of certain options. This will then develop more self-reliant and responsible inside the family and subsequently when they become adults.

These are just a few things you can do to assist your children to accept you as a single parent and start your new family life off on the right foot. You should seek information and direction from numerous sources. Internet research may provide you with a lot of ideas, but you may need to obtain some personal therapy or face-to-face talk time for your unique concerns.

You may be able to locate a support group for single parents that will be extremely beneficial. Other single parents can share with you their experiences and lessons. And you can have some support from people who do understand your situation.

Chapter 6

Ethnically Speaking: The Trends In Single Parenting

Studies reveal that 90% of all single parents are women. In 1995, roughly one-third of all black families lived in single-parent households with children. At the same time, just 8% of white families and 7% of South Asian families were single-parent homes.

About half of black women of 30 and older are the major source of income for their single-parent households, whereas just a tenth of South Asian moms are the main bread earners.

These numbers underline the hardships confronting single black moms today.

Further, other research suggests that, for both black and white women from 15 to 44, choices regarding marriage and having children are predominantly motivated by worries about family disturbance.

An ethnic research performed regarding daughters of single moms. Their results may surprise you. Daughters of solitary moms have a:

53% likelihood of marrying while teenagers
111% likelihood of having babies when they are teens
164% likelihood of having infants out of wedlock
92% likelihood of experiencing marital problems

In households where the father died early, the research led to these findings concerning daughters of single mothers:

Early loss of the father does not greatly influence black children.
Growing up in a single-parent home did not influence whether daughters will remarry after divorce whether they were black or white.

The research supports the conclusion that women who grew up in a single-parent home with their moms as heads are more likely to marry and have children when they're young, to have illegitimate children, and to have unsuccessful marriages ending in divorce. Being a single parent is challenging for anybody, regardless of race or nationality. Everyone goes through the same mourning process following the loss of a committed relationship, whether via divorce or death. Single parents have the same or comparable feelings regarding their change in status: grief, perplexity, guilt, abandonment, worry, and dread of being alone.

Here are some recommendations that, although sometimes tough to execute, may make your new life as a single parent simpler.

1. **Let go**. To go over the sentiments, it's vital to forgive and forget. Holding on to anger simply generates health issues, trouble in social interactions, and delayed emotional rehabilitation. While you may not be able to forget the wounds of the past, it's necessary to forgive and move on. Especially for the kids, you need to reconcile thoughts about your spouse so you can offer a healthy caring home for your children.

2. **Keep up with and create pals**. Looking to your neighbors and community as a source of emotional support might make all the difference while you're attempting to adapt to a new and odd lifestyle. Neighbors may give social contact, assistance for childcare, and aid with house maintenance and yard chores. Making new close-to-home friends will also help you get past feelings of abandonment and isolation and give you some critically-important relaxation and fun. Neighbors might also be quite crucial in helping your children adapt to their new situation.

3. **Give the youngsters some responsibility**. When you provide a chore to your kid, it helps them feel important and needed. It also provides them a tremendous feeling of achievement to finish the assignment

effectively. Giving your children home tasks can help improve family relationships, create self-confidence, and let your children know you need and trust them.

4. **Accept your duties**. Before you were a single parent, responsibilities for making a livelihood and taking care of the family and home were divided. Now, you're the sole adult, and you have to do everything. Don't get stuck up on feeling tricked or punished. You may not realize it, but your children will interpret your feelings as their fault. Unless you're prepared to stand up to the plate physically and emotionally, you're likely to put a gulf between you and your kids that will be extremely tough to overcome.

5. **Ask for aid**. You have to take responsibility and do the best you can with it. But recognize that you don't have

to accomplish everything by yourself. Relying more on your children for household chores and family decision-making will build a stronger family and take some of the weight off your shoulders. Relying on friends and neighbors who offer to help will reduce your stress and build your feelings of gratitude for the good things in your life. Taking the initiative and seeking out assistance from state and local governments will get you much-needed help that you're entitled to as a citizen. Never believe you're alone because you aren't.

6. **Honor ancient habits**. Both you and your children need stability at this tough time. If you used to go out for dinner every Wednesday or eat pizza every Monday, continue to do so today. If you used to go to the park every Saturday afternoon as a two-parent family, do it

now as a single-parent family. The more habits and routines you can preserve from your old way of life, the more stable and secure you're family will be in their new life.

7. **Encourage your kids to grow**. If their time is divided between parents currently, your children are experiencing their own set of obstacles and concerns to handle. The more you can do to help children extend their viewpoint and learn to cope with life's obstacles, the more equipped they will be for the future. Just like you have to go through feelings following the death of your spouse, your children have to work through their emotions. You may assist them to achieve it via open and honest dialogue. You may also assist children to increase their understanding of the world by providing them with new experiences.

Chapter 7

Financial Help For Single Parents

Being a single parent is a difficult challenge, especially when money is tight. If you're a single parent with financial problems, you may find this post useful.

Governments throughout the globe are becoming increasingly conscious of how crucial it is for a family with single parents to have a consistent source of income. They know that single parents have to make tough decisions and sacrifices to establish a safe environment for their children.

Single parents, after all, have other alternatives. Abortion is the first option to make, and single parents have opted not to take this "easy way" out of their circumstances. They have not abandoned their children or handed them up for adoption. Whether we recognize it or not, single parenting is a choice, and many single parents who make that decision are heroes.

Without proper financial means, the life of a single parent may be challenging and dismal. Struggling from day to day to offer nutritious meals is a fight. Providing adequate clothing for growing children frequently involves acceptance of hand-me-downs and garments thrown off by more privileged folks. Health insurance may be out of the question, thus free and low-cost clinics are the health care options they must pick.

If they don't have a vehicle, transportation relies on the regular functioning of often undependable public mass transit networks. And even if they do have a vehicle, frequent maintenance expenditures and repairs may make utilizing that automobile difficult. Keeping the children well-fed, warm, and healthy is a major task with many obstacles.

Yet, despite it all, they continue to trudge their path. They do everything they can to face the obstacles and offer their children as close to a normal existence as possible. Fortunately, there are organizations where single parents may seek financial support. This financial support may help reduce some of the challenges single parents encounter. Any aid is appreciated help when your children are starving. While the federal government gives some limited support, local and state governments most typically constitute the greatest option for financial aid for single parents with children at home. Unfortunately, it is often tough to qualify, but thorough study and effort may pay dividends.

Where to Find Financial Help

The greatest areas to start searching for financial aid are your county and local governments. Family service departments, children's agencies, and local unemployment services may offer financial assistance. Your state government may also have programs that will help. Start with the blue pages in your telephone book. Look for family services, health and welfare, employment/unemployment agencies, and children's welfare departments and agencies. Make a lot of phone calls to discover the offices that can assist you.

This may be an intensely frustrating exercise, as you'll get a lot of accidental hang-ups and be transferred more than you think possible. But hang in there. Keep talking to others, and eventually, you'll discover that one committed public worker who genuinely wants to assist. Get their name and preserve their phone number in case you need their services again. And thank them for their kindness. They may do it for a living, but the ones that will genuinely work for you do it from the heart.

Once you've discovered the correct office, you'll have to fill out some documents. Be prepared to spend some time doing it. Patience and tolerance are the code words. You can't get anything by being angry or unpleasant. As much as it may chafe, be nice and kind.

When you fill out all the essential paperwork, be honest. Half-truths, omissions, and blatant falsehoods can only cause disappointment later on, and they may disqualify you from support from any organization in the jurisdiction.

You'll probably have to verify your income level, occupations you have had or have currently your residence, and the number and ages of your children. Be prepared to provide income tax statements, payroll stubs, mail documenting your address, and birth certificates for you and your kids. The more paperwork you have in hand, the quicker and easier the procedure will go. You must know the prerequisites and credentials. Most financial assistance institutions have minimal income restrictions. If you more than that amount, you possibly may not qualify for support. There may be additional needs, too. You may have to qualify based on the rent you pay.

Look into the possibilities accessible to your children. Even if you don't qualify, your children could be eligible for help from school food coupons or other programs.

How Do I Know If I'm Eligible for Financial Help?

Eligibility restrictions will vary by state and by the municipal government. You'll have to do your study to figure out what's necessary for your location. But if you've already discovered the suitable agencies, the task is virtually done. The agency will have pamphlets and brochures that outline its requirements and qualifications.

Generally, there are basic requirements that all governments ask for. First, you must be single - divorced, widowed, or never married. You may not qualify if you are in a common law situation or living with someone without a marriage license.

If you are widowed, you and your children may already qualify for Social Security assistance. Contact your local Social Security Administration office for further information. Once again, brace yourself for a lengthy tiresome search. Try to find that one person who cares. They are out there, and if you make enough phone calls, you'll find them.

If you are handicapped or disabled, you may qualify for disability aid. Health departments and employment offices may be able to point you in the right direction for help with health and disability issues.

Parents whose partner is in prison may qualify for financial aid whether or not they are legally married. If you can demonstrate that your spouse can not provide funds, you may be able to get financial assistance from your state, county, or community. This will depend on where you reside. Contact your state and local law enforcement agencies to start your research. They may be able to help you ask the right questions. Again, your children may qualify for financial assistance in their rights. Look into programs that are geared toward health and welfare for children. But beware, you don't want to get in a situation where the government questions your fitness as a parent.

If you have ever had allegations or charges brought against your parenting, this may not be an appropriate answer.

What If I Can't Get Financial Help?

If your situation is dire and you still can't get help, it may be time to make some very hard choices. Perhaps you have relatives who could provide living space for a while until you can have a more stable income. Maybe your family would be willing to take one or all of your children in for a spell until you can get on your feet. As unpleasant as that choice may be, it's better than handing your children over to a government institution.

See if local churches can help. They may be able to provide meals and clothing and some medical aid. Offer to conduct duties at the church in return for aid.

If you are homeless, try local shelters. People will not let children suffer if there are any choices open to them.

Finally, if you can't seem to find the help you need, you may need to consider seeking foster care for your children.

Whatever decisions you must make, make them in the best interest of your children. And God is with you in your journey.

Chapter 8

How Many Single Parents Are Enrolled In College

Experts assume that two of every ten college students nowadays is a single parent, whether male or female. And the number of single parents in college is on a continuous climb. This shouldn't be shocking as single-parent homes have been on a rapid and steady climb for many decades. Whether by circumstance or design, single parenthood is a common lifestyle for people today.

Today, more single parents are enrolling in college than ever before. Single parents endure severe problems, and single parents who are also college students have extra stressors and obligations to cope with.

The Challenges for Single-Parent College Students

Single parents attending college face numerous challenges and problems. They have demands on their time larger than the amount of time they spend in class. They must also study to acquire excellent academic success. Pressures to succeed in class are added to those they already feel from their home and child-rearing obligations.

Society may not acknowledge the increased hardship. Being a single parent in college doesn't reduce societal expectations for having parent-teacher conferences, attending PTA meetings, coaching kids' sports teams, and the myriad of activities required of parents nowadays.

And others may regard single parents in college differently. Even if having children was a deliberate decision, others may infer that the single parent was reckless in his or her social and sexual activities. Peers and professors may assume the single parent is promiscuous, creating even more problems for the married student. So although the stigma against single parents has mostly evaporated in contemporary western countries, it may not be fully gone for single parents in college.

Managing Time

Handling busy schedules and fulfilling tough time limitations is challenging enough for single parents. There are so many expectations and demands, and the same 24 hours for achieving them. For the single parent attending college, time is a valuable asset. They must in some way cope with the need to study and keep up their grades with the need to take care of their children and offer them a pleasant, healthy environment in which to develop. Class attendance and the children's extra-curricular activities may collide.

Exams may be scheduled over soccer games. They may have to pick between bringing the infant to the pediatrician and going to their doctor for that severe cold. There are no simple alternatives for single parents in college.

Time limits influence more than the kids and family unit. The single-parent college student has little time to care for their own physical and mental well-being. Getting regular exercise, a good diet, and appropriate rest may be difficult.

Finding the time and a quiet place to study may be one of the most difficult parts of their day. Often, the study doesn't begin until after the kids are asleep. That means missing crucial hours of their sleep. Balancing academic life and a single-parent household are a Herculean effort.

managing money

Single parents already confront the problem of being the primary source of income for their family. Attending college adds a significant financial burden to an already strained pocketbook and budget.

As most of us know, college expenses are significant today. The costs of tuition and fees, textbooks, laboratory fees, and transportation and parking eat into limited money for rent, groceries, and child care.

While student loans are available, they add to financial burdens unknown to college students who don't have children. Mounting debt may be a necessary evil for single parents attending college.

Is there any question, then, about why so many single parents drop out of college or get failing grades? Recent studies suggest that some single parents are choosing to put their kids in foster care or out for adoption to improve their lives with a college degree. Those without a supportive extended family or outside resources may be forced to make this heartbreaking decision to give their children the best possible chance at life. The hard fact of the matter is that, without a college degree, single parents may not be able to give their children a normal life anyway.

No matter how tempted we may be to judge the single parent in college who gives up their children, it is important to recognize and acknowledge their terrible dilemma. And for those that can pull it off, society owes a round of thunderous applause.

Chapter 9

Meeting Single Parents

Even when you knew it was coming, being a single parent may be an unexpected shock. A few years off of the dating world, and you forget how to do it. Don't feel different. It's never easy to date, and dating as a newly single mom is a particular hardship.

It's been years since you dressed up and went out with someone for a lovely evening. You've forgotten what to say and what to do. You feel uncomfortable and clumsy. You may have put on a few pounds or gained some new grey hairs. Let's face it, you're afraid.

Well, dating isn't simple - even for singles without kids. It's hard to meet people. It's hard to determine whether someone's safe and reliable. You never know what you'll receive until you walk out, and then you're trapped - at least for an hour or two. Dating's simply not the devil-may-care pleasure some people hype it out to be.

To feel comfortable with dating, you have to have been dating for a long. You have to build up your dating repertoire. You have to train those social and emotional "dating muscles," muscles that readily atrophy without frequent usage.

But don't worry. It'll be all right. All you need is some refreshers to get back into the dating game. A short talk, a cup of coffee, a stroll in the park - all you need is a few easy victories to restore confidence and tone those atrophied dating muscles. After some experience and a few great dates, you'll be back in the flow of things.

Before you start dating again, however, you'll want to do some internal work - you'll want to get yourself in top dating form. Here are some suggestions that may get you off to the perfect start.

Tie up loose ends.

Before you start dating and becoming engaged in new relationships, you want to be sure that your past is your past. If you're still hurting from rejection, abandonment, or catastrophic loss, you need to allow yourself time to mourn and recover. It takes around a year for individuals to go through the regular mourning process, so don't push yourself. And if there are financial concerns still up in the air, have them handled and done. You don't want to start dating while you're still trying to work out financial and legal details. Once you've gone through the bereavement process and addressed business affairs, it's time to move on with your life.

Understand your motives.

Why do you want to date again? Is it because your best buddy believes you should? The only decent reason to date is because you want to. Maybe you want basic company and someone to do things with. It's acceptable if you're not ready to embark on a committed relationship. You probably shouldn't yet.

Are you that lonely that you'd go out with anyone? Loneliness isn't a valid cause for dating either. If you're so desperate that you'll say yes to the first one that comes along, you're putting yourself up for disappointment, annoyance, and heartbreak. When you date, it's because you want to spend time with another person. After all, you like them and want to know them better. Unless you're interested in a future date, drop it.

When you want to date because you need time to relax with an intriguing individual, it's time to start dating.

Get your life in order.

Single parents have distinct obligations and expectations. You have to balance the need to earn a living with the need to raise happy healthy children. There may seem to be little or no time left over for dating.

That's why it's crucial to identify your priorities and put up a schedule. Planning to attend school activities, putting in those additional hours at work, and having some social life is crucial. As a single parent, those spur-of-the-moment dates are most certainly impossible. Recognize the constraints and adapt your expectations.

You'll be a far more fascinating date if you're not thinking about yesterday's laundry or tomorrow's meals. When you have the opportunity to go out for a wonderful romantic evening, you don't want to be obsessed with the tasks and problems of the day. It's your time to relax and have fun. Having and maintaining a regular schedule can help you achieve that.

You'll also need to arrange for babysitters, let people know where you'll be and when you'll be back, and carry a cell phone with you for emergencies. Daters who are not also parents may not have those needs. These are things you can't jump into. You need a prior warning to set your life in order and be ready to relax and have fun on your important day.

Stay Interested to Stay Interesting

Even though your schedule is tight and your days are full, you need to be a well-rounded person to be an interesting date. Be sure to take personal time and keep your mind active despite the household chaos. Read a book. Go to a lecture. Take the kids to a museum. Learn something new. Take on a new hobby that your kids will enjoy too. Making personal growth a family affair can't be a losing proposition.

Maintain your friendships and family relationships. Even if you're not dating, it's important to have social contact with other adults. Invite your friends or family over for supper or negotiate an invitation to go to their place. Plan some adult-only activities so that you can have adult talks and stay up with current events. Stay active.

Take care of your health. Find ways to get regular exercise. Walks with the kids, visits to the local park or nature preserve, and workouts will keep you fit and healthy. You've got a lot of stress in your life, and exercise will help work that stresses off and out. You'll be a more calm human being if you are a healthy human being.

Life as a single parent may arrive quickly, without notice. Even though you know it's coming, it's a shock when your entire life changes. When you have children, such changes come with hefty loads and challenging obstacles.

Returning to the dating environment may be a terrifying experience, but you can learn to love dating when you take the measures required to develop a strong, secure lifestyle and family.

Chapter 10

Single Parents Dating: It Is Time To Move On

Becoming a single parent isn't an end. It's a beginning. Your new lifestyle is full of duty and difficulties. It may be more important now than ever that you find time for yourself. You need to relax and have fun. It may have been a while, but you may date now.

You may not be ready to get into a new relationship, but that doesn't mean you can't go out and have a wonderful time with friends. Dating old friends is a terrific way to re-enter the single world and revive old friendships. They already know you, and they're easy to chat with. You need someone now to speak to and to seek guidance. Old acquaintances may also be a source of support around the home or at work.

But if you're interested in meeting new people and entering into a more serious relationship, you may want to try some real-life dating. But dating as a newly single parent might provide unique obstacles. Demands on your time may already be enormous.

Taking care of the kids, earning a job, and keeping your home are time-consuming duties. That makes it even more crucial to make time for your enjoyment and relaxation. But time management skills will undoubtedly be essential to prevent your life from becoming hectic and unpleasant.

You may be emotionally raw at this time. Whether you've lost your spouse via separation, divorce, or death, you're going through some incredibly huge life changes. You need to be cautious not to leap into the first relationship that comes along. You need to have fun, but you also need some time to recuperate and become independent again.

Here are some things to consider:

Am I ready to date yet?

Re-entering the solitary scene might be unsettling. You may not feel self-confident about your appearance, or you may feel that you've lost some crucial social abilities. But fear of dating shouldn't be a determining factor. Sooner or later, you're going to have to take that major step to have a regular life again.

There are some things to think about, however. You're going through a challenging moment, and you may feel emotionally sensitive and confused. You may not have the discernment to perceive your dates' shortcomings. You must take care to safeguard yourself and your children from predators and persons that will use you.

Are you prepared to tell your children you're dating? Your kids are also going through a significant shift, and they may feel insecure or envious if a new adult is brought to the household. Have you prepared them for this? Do they understand your emotions and support you? If your children aren't ready for you to date, you may not be. But there's a limit. The main thing is, to be honest, and transparent with them about what you need and desire. After all, they aren't dating the individual. You are. Just keep the lines of communication open and transparent.

Getting into relationships too soon is a typical error for newly-single parents. You're used to being part of a relationship and feel uneasy and self-conscious going out alone. You may not be done with the past relationship. Losing a spouse, no matter how necessitates going through a mourning process to recover emotionally and re-establish a regular life. Studies reveal that it takes at least a year for individuals to comprehend their loss and move on. Be sure you've allowed yourself enough time to heal.

You may also need to wrap up loose ends from the prior relationship. There may be financial and legal concerns remaining pending that must be closed. If your spouse died away, you'll need to settle the estate, dispose of possessions, and complete insurance concerns. Better to concentrate on the work at hand while you're mourning than to inject a new complication into an already- complex existence.

You also need to take time to assist your children to mourn the loss. They may be feeling abandoned, and they'll need your love, support, and encouragement to go ahead. And they need to develop a new connection with you, one where you're the sole parent. Dating too soon might defraud them of this critical time with you and develop behavioral issues that are not simple to overcome. Take it gradually for their sake and yours.

Chapter 11

How Do Single Parents Find People To Date?

It's undoubtedly been a long time since you were in the dating environment, and you may have lost contact with your single friends and hobbies. One approach to meeting new people is via your pals. Perhaps your closest buddy knows someone they believe would be great for you. Take a risk. Go on a blind date.

You also have a restriction that many singles don't: time. You must schedule your social activities well in advance so you can obtain a babysitter or make other arrangements for your children. So, everything you do to meet new people can't be a spur-of-the-moment decision.

Many places feature singles organizations where you may meet other unattached individuals. As long as you don't have to make commitments, this is a terrific method to meet people. Group social activities are entertaining and safe. You have an opportunity to get to know them before being alone with them.

You may even be able to discover social groups exclusively for single parents. This way, you'll encounter folks whose lives are more like yours. They share the same issues and problems. You may find it easier to connect to another single parent, and surely they will be more understanding when something comes up at the last minute.

What about relationships?

You are the only person who knows if you're ready to start a serious relationship. Of course, you are not alone, and your children will influence your readiness and willingness to get into a relationship.

You need to be very clear in your mind about where you are and what you want. Perhaps you only want companionship and social contact. If you're not ready to get serious, let your dates know. Don't allow yourself to become more involved than you can handle emotionally.

Your first few dates shouldn't be serious, and you don't need to involve your children in your casual dates. But if you're lonely and feel you need someone to love, you may be more interested in getting serious. First, you must ask yourself why. Getting into a serious relationship because you're lonely isn't a great idea. You want to become connected with a person, not merely fill a space in your life. Be aware of your motivations before you allow things to grow too serious.

What to do when on a date?

You'll want to know that your dates will be both entertaining and safe. Your family relies on you, and taking risks to date isn't appropriate. Always be sure someone knows where you're going and who you're going with. Let them know when you'll be home, and take your cell phone with you in case of an emergency. Let your date know about your family and that you might get a call. No surprises are a good policy.

When you go out, you'll want to do something that helps you get to know each other. Look for places where you can talk and activities that encourage conversation and interaction. Movies aren't a good idea for those first few dates because they don't provide a good get-to-know-you environment. Better to go bowling or play miniature golf than to go to a movie.

For first dates especially, you must go to public places. Your safety is very important, and you don't want to take chances with people you don't know. You might even want to arrange to meet your date somewhere so that you aren't dependent on them for your ride home.

Chapter 12

Effective Vacation Tours For Single Parents

Single parents often become overwhelmed with the high burden of responsibilities and time demands that come with being the sole adult in a family. Concerns about money, child upbringing, and personal health loom big, and solitary parents may overlook their own needs for leisure and enjoyment.

If you're a single parent feeling burdened down by too much to do and not enough time, maybe it's time for you to consider taking a vacation tour for single-parent families. Everyone needs the occasional vacation, and single parents are no exception to the rule.

A vacation tour for single-parent families gives time to renew and rejuvenate your mind and body and the possibility to get closer to your children in a new environment. It's a family adventure you'll share for years to come.

Single parents have their burdens, and children in single-parent families have their problems, too. They often feel neglected or abandoned by a busy single parent that has to go to work and care for the household. They get little bits of time from their parent and sometimes end up spending much of their time with other caretakers. A vacation tour for single-parent families gives them the chance to be with their single parents in a whole new way.

Vacation tours for single-parent families help you rebuild strained relations with your children. You won't be answering those phone calls from the boss, meeting with professional colleagues or your kids' teachers, and you won't have to deal with the thousands of daily interruptions that keep you and your children at odds.

The community of single-parent families is growing so rapidly that most travel agencies have vacation tours specifically for single-parent families. They'll arrange for travel by train, plane, or cruise ship and help your family comply with international travel requirements when necessary.

Of all, you can't simply pack up and leave on a vacation tour for single-parent families. You'll need to plan your vacation several months in advance to get the best prices and accommodations. A good rule of thumb is to book your vacation tour for single-parent families at least two months before the departure date.

If you don't have passports or visas, you'll need to allow a little more time for government processes to work to assure you have the necessary papers. Your travel agent should be able to tell you what the country you're visiting requires and help you get the paperwork started. If you're using a travel agent who specializes in vacation tours for single-parent families, they should be able to help you with almost everything you'll need including travel, hotel accommodations, tickets to special events and entertainment areas, and restaurants that cater to children.

Of course, vacation excursions for single-parent families are accessible inside the United States where you don't have to bother about passports and visas.

They're easy to arrange and don't demand as much advance time for bookings. Wherever you decide to go, you can learn a lot about your location by visiting the official website and travel-related sites that provide information and travel reviews that can help you figure out what you want to do when you get there. You may also give the country's embassy a call to obtain additional information about things to see and do, and letting them know you're a single parent with children may be useful.

Travel businesses that specialize in holiday trips for single-parent families should be more knowledgeable and mindful of your specific requirements than other agencies. They should recognize your time limits and relieve you of as much of the preparation as feasible. They should also be experienced dealing with youngsters on holiday excursions for single-parent families.

Some prominent firms are supporting vacation trips for single-parent families in their workplaces. They may provide the vacation as a bonus for great achievement or as a specific incentive for future success.

If you work at a large corporation, you might check with the personnel office to see if your company has or is planning this great service. Signing up for a vacation tour for single-parent families is the best favor you can do for yourself and your kids. You all struggle with strains and demands every day. You more than deserve a decent vacation, you need it! Taking the kids on a holiday tour for single-parent families provides you with all healthy sunlight and fresh air, brings you together as a family and gives you memories that will last a lifetime.

www.ingramcontent.com/pod-product-compliance
Lightning Source LLC
LaVergne TN
LVHW050327160826
845677LV00014B/3560

* 9 7 9 8 8 4 6 8 1 4 2 8 8 *